DATE DUE			

Aren't You Glad!

Aren't You Glad!

✲✲✲

HELEN LOWRIE MARSHALL

Illustrated by Ed Nuckolls

Doubleday & Company, Inc., Garden City, New York

1973

Dedicated to
People Helping People

ISBN: 0-385-06748-8
Library of Congress Catalog Card Number 73–79694
Copyright © 1973 by Helen Lowrie Marshall
All Rights Reserved
Printed in the United States of America
First Edition

Contents

Aren't You Glad!

In this miracle world we live in
    Of dreams beyond dreams come true,
Isn't it great to be alive!
    And aren't you glad you're you!

Aren't you proud to be meeting
    The challenge of today,
And to know in your heart that you've a part
    That nobody else can play?

Aren't you glad that you are free,
    With a chance to prove your powers
As a child of God and a loyal son
    Of this glorious land of ours?

Marching along to the stirring beat
    Of the drums in the Big Parade,
In step with life and in tune with the times,
    Joyous and unafraid!

In this wonder-filled world we live in—
    This world riding high on a star—
Aren't you thrilled to be alive
    And to be the person you are!

Live It Up!

Live it *up*—not down—
Wear a smile—not a frown—
It's a glorious time to be living!
Find joy in the day
And give some away—
Joy doubles itself in the giving.
Be glad you are you—
Make others glad, too.
Hold up your heart like a cup
Till its joy overflows
And all the world knows
You're glad you're alive—
    Live it up!

It's a Fact

You can put the art of pretending
To work for you. It's a fact,
If you act the way you would like to be,
You'll soon be the way you act.

Tryst with Life

I railed at the circumstances
    That would not let me grow
And reach the goal I had set for myself
    In the way I had hoped to go.

Then at my feet I saw it—
    A small green growing thing,
Pushing its way through the pavement
    In tryst with life and spring.

The forces of God and Nature
    Revealed in a blade of grass,
Stubbornly pitting its fragile strength
    Against that immutable mass.

A blade of grass in the pavement—
    But I suddenly wanted to leap—
Come what may, I would find a way,
    I, too, had a tryst to keep!

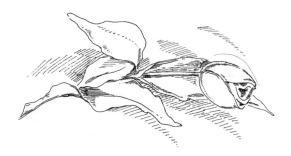

A Dream Is Now

A dream should not be a withdrawal—
  A hiding from life away;
A dream should inspire the dreamer
  To live with purpose each day.

The dream brings the future in focus,
  But more it can never do,
Unless each immediate task be done
  Toward making that dream come true,

Unless every day we are willing
  To tackle the job at hand
With all of the strength and talent and zest
  We have at our command.

A dream should point to improvement,
  Not flight from reality;
It should be an urge to discover
  The best that our life can be.

It should reach for a deeper involvement
  In life toward a definite goal,
A search for a broader meaning—
  A life that is rich and whole.

Castles in the Air

You say that your castles
        Are all in the air.
Well, don't be discouraged
        Because they are there.
Dream-fashioned castles
        Are nebulous things,
Fragile and fleeting
        As butterfly wings;
But every castle come true
        Had its start
In dreams like your own
        That began in the heart.

The dream must come first,
        Then, if it has worth,
You find ways to build
        Its foundations on earth.
So if you've a castle
        Still floating in air,
Remember that castles
        And dreams belong there.
But if you would make it
        Become real and sound,
You'll sink its foundations
        In deep, solid ground.

Build on Truth

Build your life on truth today
And there will be no fears
Enveloping your thoughts of future
Days and coming years.
      Make each day an open, honest
      Day with no pretense
      And you will never feel the need
      Of cringing self-defense.
Face life squarely, build on truth,
Let no deceit degrade,
And you will face death, too, in time,
Undaunted, unafraid.

Only One Failure

There is only one failure
      We need to fear—
To be untrue to our best;
To fail to exert all the strength
      That is ours
And give it the utmost test.
Only one failure we need to dread—
      That we be content to be
Less than our best—to be satisfied
      With our own mediocrity.

Joyous and Unafraid

I would face life on my own terms,
    Joyous and unafraid,
Seeing each task, however small,
    As a plan divinely made.

I would meet life as an old friend,
    Worthy my trust and love;
Grateful for such a gracious gift
    Given me from above.

I would see life as a teacher,
    With lessons that I must learn,
Honestly proud of such rewards
    As my own efforts may earn.

I would face life as adventure,
    Each glorious day sun-rayed,
To be met with a faith in the ultimate good,
    Joyous and unafraid!

Look for a Star

There is a star—a special star
    That shines for you alone,
A star whose beams are made of dreams
    That you, alone, have known.

A star whose light, though clouds of night
    May threaten to obscure,
Will light the way with steady ray
    And guide you, safe and sure.

Look for that star—look high and far,
    And keep it well in view,
That star with beams of secret dreams
    That no one knows but you.

Up to Me

I know that God loves me
    In spite of my faults;
Of this I have never a doubt.
But whether He *likes* me or not—
    There's a point
That I can do something about.

Ride the High Winds!

Ride the high winds! Rise above
    The petty and the small;
Know the thrill of living,
    The wonder of it all!

Let your soul break through the clouds
    To where the skies are blue;
Let your dreams be airborne
    Till you catch that wider view.

Ride the high winds! Lift your sights,
    Break those restraining bars;
Dare the sky! You can, if you try,
    Reach out and touch the stars!

Character

Character is a home-grown thing,
  Nurtured in heart and mind;
Fed by the showers and sunshine
  Of thoughts that are there consigned.

Rooted in loam that amasses
  All of our growing years,
The richness of love and of laughter,
  The rains of the heartaches and tears.

Character is a slow-grown thing
  That grows from our life within—
The thoughts we think and the deeds we do
  And the will that we have to win.

Aware

How wonderful if we could be
  Aware for just one hour
Of every lovely thing around,
  Each tree and bird and flower;
Each friend and every loved one,
  And how much we really care—
How splendid if, for one short hour,
  We all might be aware.

Going Somewhere?

Are you going somewhere, young friend of mine?
Are you heading for some destination?
Is there a goal you alone can see,
Worthy of your dedication?

Or are you drifting aimlessly,
Confused by each detour sign,
Giving yourself to the will of the wind?
Where do you go, friend of mine?

The end of the road comes all too soon;
Will it find you triumphant there,
Looking back on a journey of days well lived
With your soul still alive and aware?

Are you going somewhere, young friend of mine?
God speed you on your way,
With a goal in view and the heart of you
Strong for each coming day.

Memories, Memories

I wonder what nostalgic thoughts
Will bring the smiles and tears
When these young rebels of our time
Have reached the harvest years.

Will they remember how the family
Gathered every night
To watch, in silence, TV actors
Brawl and curse and fight?

Will they recall the sitters
When Mom was at some meeting,
And all those luscious TV dinners
They were always eating?

And when their children criticize
The way the country's going,
Will they attempt to cover up
And keep their sons from knowing,

Or will they boast about
Those good old bygone days when laws
Were something to be broken,
No matter what the cause;

When they marched with obscene signs,
Burned schools and churches down,
And dressed in dirty, ragged clothes
Like some hobo or clown?

When they have children of their own,
Will they be heard to brag
How they destroyed their draft cards
And burned their country's flag?

Will they recall the "trips" they took,
How they dropped out of school,
And how the only thing in life
Was just to "keep it cool?"

I wonder what their memories
Will hold down through the years,
And whether their remembering
Will bring them smiles or tears.

A Choice

Profanity is real
        But so is prayer;
Those who harbor hate
        And those who care;
Ugliness is real,
        But so is beauty;
Those who give from love,
        And those from duty.
The shady side exists,
        That we admit,
But there's a sunny side
        Offsetting it.
The thing for which we all
        Ought to rejoice
Is that the good Lord
        Gives us each a choice.

The Longest Journey

Life's longest, most difficult journey
Is the quest in search of ourselves.
We may glean an abundance of knowledge
From books upon the shelves,
May visit the ports of every land
From pole to the farthest pole,
But our questing journey can never end
Till we face up to our soul;

Till we explore the workings
Of the mind that rules inside,
And study all the sources
Of our humbleness and pride;
Till we admit our weaknesses
And recognize our strength,
And take an honest measure
Of our soul's true height and length.

A long, hard journey, but the most
Rewarding one, by far—
Leading us to see ourselves
As the person we really are.

Growth

When we were small, our father
Used to mark our height each year
Upon our old home's doorframe;
Those old markings still are clear.

How proud he was to see how much
We'd grown since last birthday.
"You'll be a man before we know it,"
He would proudly say.

We're older now, and no more
Penciled lines show how we've grown,
As we stand where those marks were made
And once so proudly shown.

I wonder if the measure
Of our soul on Heaven's door
Marks greater heights attained each year
Beyond the year before,

And if our Heavenly Father
Is ever heard to say,
With honest pride, "Well done, my son,
You'll be a man some day."

Milestones

Walking home from country school—
    How clearly I recall—
The long miles seemed so endless
    If I thought about them all;
So I would look on up the road
    And choose a stone or tree,
A distance short enough so I
    Could reach it easily.
And, after that, another mark,
    And so on, all the way,
Until the miles were covered
    With an ease almost like play.

Sometimes the dream goal of our life
    Seems such a long, long way.
I find that childhood game of mine
    Works just as well today.
I set my sights upon a smaller goal
    Within my reach,
And keep on setting further marks
    As I attain to each.
The far-off dream draws closer
    With each victory won, I find,
And life's a game again with every
    Milestone left behind.

Uncle Gus

Quite a fellow, Uncle Gus,
No blood kin to any of us,
But we called him "Uncle" and thought of him so,
The kind of relationship small towns know.
He'd swap a yarn at the drop of a hat,
And, naturally, all of us kids loved that.
Born of the prairies, rawboned and lank,
He'd sit on a bench in front of the bank
And tell us tales of the early days,
Modestly spiced with great self-praise
That made him a hero in our eyes.
He was a great one to dramatize
The commonplace and make it seem
The height of every small boy's dream.
No one could equal Uncle Gus
For making life adventurous.

And, though his earthly means were small,
He left a legacy to us all—
His eyes, that through them we might see
How truly glorious life can be;
His heart, that we might better meet
Life's battles with a steadier beat;
And, best of all, dreams left to grow
In the minds of those youngsters he loved so.

Talk About Miracles

We talked about miracles, Charlie and I,
Sipping our coffee, eating our pie,
Wondering idly, if, where and when
Man would be privileged to see one again.

I lost a portion of what Charlie said,
For one of those giant jets zoomed overhead,
And the TV was blaring, too loudly by far,
With pictures from Africa bounced off a star.

And the pie and the coffee were changed, as we sat,
To ideas and energy, blood, bone and fat,
And the words that we spoke, memory filed them away
In case we might want to recall them someday.

We finished our coffee and settled the bill
And went back to work, idly wondering still
If mankind ever again would behold
Miracles such as the Bible told.

The Old Man with the Cup

Rain or shine, we'd see him sitting
    In his little kingdom there—
A patch of city sidewalk,
    Maybe three or four feet square.

There he sat throughout the seasons
    With his dog beside him curled,
The proud, respected ruler
    Of his corner of the world.

And when he said "Good morning"
    There was something in his smile
That made you know that it *was* good,
    And living *was* worthwhile.

He seemed to have a bit of sun
    That he had tucked away
To use especially on days
    When skies were cold and gray.

He made the day seem cleaner, brighter,
    Made your soul look up—
We'll miss him on the corner there,
    The old man with the cup.

The Touch of Life on Life

I look in the mirror, and what do I see?
Myriad faces look back at me,
So many others that helped to define
That one in the mirror I dare to call mine.

So many other lives crossed with my own,
More than I've ever consciously known,
Leaving their mark in some degree
On that in the mirror that I call me.

So many gratitude debts I owe,
More than I ever can possibly know,
So many helpers along my way,
So many debts I can never repay.

I look in the mirror and what do I see?
A lifetime of faces looking at me,
A lifetime of lives that helped to design
That one in the mirror I dare to call mine.

The Secret

He simply didn't know how to quit,
And that, no doubt, was the secret of it—
His power, his fortune, his fame and success,
The way he enjoyed life and spread happiness.
He never spent time looking back with regret,
But said of each problem, "I'll conquer it yet."
And conquer he did, for he never gave up.
If his cup runneth over, he molded that cup!
He had faith in God and a joy in all living,
A generous hand and a way of forgiving.
He had his misfortunes, his worries, his grief,
But he held to his ideals, his faith, his belief.
He won a good life with his will and his wit,
And the fact that he just didn't know how to quit.

A Basic Life

I would have a basic life
  Made up in simple line
Of sturdy stuff of faith and trust,
  Its pattern, love's design.

A life that I can deck at times
  With laughter bright and gay,
Or wear with dignity the veil
  When sorrow comes my way.

A basic life of simple joys,
  A life to bear the strain
Of cheery times and tear-filled times,
  Of happiness and pain.

I would have a basic life
  Of good and graceful line,
A plain and unpretentious life
  With love its whole design.

Candles of Understanding

So human it is to misunderstand,
To judge by the outward signs,
To interpret the actions of others
By our own life's narrow confines.

But deep in our heart, if we will it,
A candle is waiting there—
The candle of understanding
To be lit by the power of prayer.

A candle of understanding
To lighten our self-dimmed mind
To know and appreciate others—
To see, where once we were blind.

The amazing thing is the love light
That one small flame can give
To warm and brighten and make this world
A happier place to live.

Believe in Spring

Do you believe in spring? Does something
    Deep within you know
That fresh, new loveliness is sleeping
    Underneath the snow?

Have you ever had the feeling
    That spring is in the air,
Even though the grip of winter closes
    Round you everywhere?

Do you believe birds will return
    And bees and butterflies
Will fly again beneath the warmth
    Of sunny, cloudless skies?

Do you believe in beauty bursting
    From a simple pod?
Then you believe in spring, and you
    Believe in life—and God.

One Small Star

Are you staggered by the cries for help,
The outstretched hands that plead?
There is so little one can do
To fill the world's great need.

A penny here—a penny there—
What good can come from such?
Yet small gifts given from the heart
Can help so very much.

And you and I with gifts of love,
All humble though they are,
Can bring to someone's night at least
The light of one small star.

Did I Betray My Lord?

Did I betray my Lord today?
Dear God, could it be I?

Could He have been the beggar
On the street that I passed by?
Was His the silent call for help
I heard but did not heed?

Were His the hands that I ignored
Held out to me in need?
Were His the causes I declined
Because I had no time
To spare in helping rid His world
Of ignorance and crime?

I'd rather not become involved,
I'd my own life to live.
Others who liked that sort of thing
Had so much more to give.
There was not time enough, I said,
And begging should be barred.
Someone should see the poor were fed;
Why should my day be marred
By such unpleasant incidents?—
And so I turned away.

Dear God, forgive me—it *was* I
Betrayed my Lord today.

Heaven's Seasons

If Heaven has a springtime—
(Could it be Heaven without?)
Then she, who's gone to live there
Must surely be about
Her springtime chores of readying
A bit of ground somewhere.
If it be Heaven for her
She must have a garden there.

If Heaven has a summertime,
Warm sun and summer showers,
Then she, who loved her garden so,
Must move among the flowers
And touch with gentle fingertips
A marigold or rose.
If Heaven's to be Heaven
It must have something that grows.

If Heaven has an autumn time,
With lazy, hazy days—
Then she, who loved the changing leaves,
Must stroll down Heaven's ways
And revel in the reds and golds
Of summer's long farewell.
If it be Heaven it must have
This time she loved so well.

If Heaven has a wintertime—
Soft white as angel wings,
Then she, who saw God's handiwork
And beauty in all things,
Must laugh aloud to see the snow
Make Heaven itself more fair.
Sure, Heaven can't be Heaven
Without the seasons there.

The Singing Winds

There's music in the stillness of the hills,
The singing winds flow softly through the trees;
My listening soul responds with silent song,
A changing mood with every passing breeze.

The whole great symphony of life is there,
The gentle lullaby, the song of love,
The fury of life's passions, grief and care,
The hymn of reverence to God above.

The harmony of nature fills the air,
Revealed in bird and tree and bursting pod,
And, listening, my singing heart responds
In joyous tune with life and love and God.

Small Growing Things

There's something in small growing things
A special satisfaction brings.
Before they even blossom wide
A gardener has a love inside
For every small, green, struggling bit
That looks to him to care for it.

There's something in small growing things
A garden just beginning brings.
Coaxing beauty from the sod
Makes a man close kin to God.

Simple Miracle

I looked upon a miracle today,
A simple act of Nature, one might say,
Yet past the skill of scientific minds,
Beyond the realm of reason where one finds
The answers to the man-made things we see;
A miracle of such simplicity—
A tender seedling bursting from its pod,
Yet seeing it, I saw the face of God.

Lilac Time

It's almost lilac time again—
    The old bush by the gate
Looks as if its heavy clustered buds
    Can hardly wait.

One day soon they'll open
    Tiny purple fists and fling
Their heavenly fragrance to the winds
    And herald in the spring.

And passers-by will smile and sense
    A glad renewal there,
For lilacs have a way of spreading
    Gladness in the air.

It's almost lilac time again—
    Each year I watch and wait
To see spring's purple banners on
    The old bush by the gate.

And every year their sweet perfume
    Is like a breath of Heaven.
No wealth on earth could buy the joy
    That lilac bush has given.

Autumn Reverie

The garden wears an air of reverie,
A tranquil, dreamy look, brown edged and dry,
As though it rests in gentle meditation
And memories of summer days gone by.

There is a quiet air of deep content;
It knows, I think, its day is almost done.
In simple tune with Nature's own fulfillment
It rests beneath the cooling autumn sun.

Its seeds of resurrection lie about;
The winter snows will fall, life will go on;
The barren stalks will bud with fresh new beauty
And spring will come as surely as the dawn.

A waiting stillness hovers over all,
And, as I touch the fern's last withered frond,
My garden tells me all I've need of knowing
Of life and death and God and Heaven beyond.

The Value of a Rose

The value of a rose? No one can say.
As well to price a perfect summer day.
From out its lowly thorn-encumbered bed,
It lifts its lovely, proud, triumphant head;
That man—himself a thorn-surrounded soul—
May know the beauty of a life made whole.

The value of a rose? Not you nor I
Can name its price. We can, at best, but try
To place its value and declare its worth
In blundering man-made terms of wealth on earth,
While angels must look on in wonder there
To see a price tag on a gift so rare.

A Special Trust

I have a special place on earth,
A special purpose, special worth,
A special reason now for being,
A joy in life past all foreseeing;
A very special gift is mine,
A special trust from One Divine—
For I know what it is to be
A friend to one who's friend to me.

And It Was Good

It must have been a day
Such as this—
The earth responding
To the sun's warm kiss,
The drone of tiny creatures,
And the breeze
Whispering happy secrets
To the trees;
The gentle stream's
Soft murmur of content—
It must have been
A day like this was meant
When writers of the Good Book
Said God stood
And looked upon His world
And found it good.

Eternal Good

There's something that's eternal
  In the quality of good,
Something infinite in nature
  Making life go as it should.

There's a deep abiding substance
    In all things right and fair;
Beauty, honesty and truth
    Are rooted everywhere.

There's something indestructible,
    The foe of every sin,
In the good that reaches outward
    From man's innate good within.

Grief

Grief is a guest, uninvited,
To be dealt with each in his way;
And which of the ways is proper or best
No one can rightfully say.

One hides his grief under laughter,
Another veils out the light;
And who's to say which is better,
And who's to say which is right?

For grief is the heart's secret burden
That time only can abate,
And each must carry in his own way
The force of its crushing weight.

A Friend Is—

What is a friend?
      Well, I would say first
He's one who still loves you
      When you're at your worst;
He's one who looks right through
      That mask that you wear,
And sees the real you
      That you thought hidden there.
He's one who believes in you
      No matter what,
And often sees virtues
      Where virtues are not.
He's one who upbraids you
      When that's what you need;
He's one quick to praise you
      And help you succeed.
A friend? Often priceless,
      Sometimes a pest,
But blessing-wise, I'd say
      He ranks with the best.

Just a Smile Away

When tears and dismal thinking
Are clouding up your day,
Remember that a miracle
Is just a smile away.

Try smiling through your tears
And watch the miracle begin—
Watch the fears retreat before
A bravely lifted chin.

Watch how faith grows firmer,
One's courage to renew.
Trying smiling through your tears and see
What just one smile will do.

The first faint rays of hope will reach
Into your darkened day—
The healing miracle begun—
And just a smile away.

Hope Is!

Hope is the soothing balm of sleep
    To heavy-laden eyes;
Hope is the arch of the rainbow
    Across gray-clouded skies.

Hope is that first fat robin
    That says spring's on its way.
Hope is the peace of twilight
    At the close of a busy day.

Hope is—and was—and will be,
    For always hope lives on,
Defeating fear in the hearts of men
    As dark is defeated by dawn.

Hope is the folded flower
    Asleep in the heart of a pod;
Hope is the candlelight of faith
    Lit by the hand of God.

Insight and Farsight

Prayer is a mirror wherein we see
Ourselves and our world within;
Our secret longings, dearest loves,
The bent we have to sin;
Our needs and daily blessings,
Our weaknesses, our strength,
Our own soul's honest measurement—
Its height and depth and length.

And prayer, too, is a window
That shows the world outside.
We sense the greatness of God's hand,
How high, how deep, how wide;
A window where we stand and watch
Our brothers passing there
And ease their heavy burdens
As we lift them up in prayer.

A mirror and a window—
Both reveal in countless ways
The insight and the farsight
That are his who truly prays.

A Faith That Holds

Dear God, give us a faith with *holding power*,
Not just a faith that blooms when life's a-flower,
Not just a faith that answers duty's call,
But faith that finds its way to cover all—
The sunny days that rouse a grateful heart,
The cloudy days, of every life a part,
The stark, black days when everything seems gone—
Dear God, give us a faith to carry on,
Our hand in Thine with grasp so firm and tight
That it will hold through all—the wrong, the right—
Knowing that every day Thy love enfolds.
Dear God, give us, we pray, a faith that holds.

For Goodness' Sake

Be a do-gooder now and then
    As therapy for your soul.
It's only the person who gives of himself
    Who ever is really whole.

For goodness' sake, do something
    And for goodness' sake alone,
And you'll be amazed at the joy it will bring,
    The greatest you've ever known.

Let Go—Let God

Have you ever tried praying about it,
    That problem that clouds your day?
Have you ever tried turning it over to God
    And letting Him have His way?

Have you ever tried saying, "Thy will be done"
    And practiced just letting go,
Knowing He'll guide you out of the fog
    Of that problem that troubles you so?

You'll find He is ready to help you,
    You need only open your heart;
He's waiting and willing to carry the load—
    The "letting go" is your part.

Work Your Worries Away

When things go wrong and days are long
    And shadows hang about,
Sometimes it helps to scrub a floor
    Or clean a closet out.

Hoe the garden, pull some weeds,
    Or bake a cake or pie.
There's nothing like a little work
    To make the hours fly.

Nothing like combating thoughts
    That dwell on fears and doubt,
By homely chores that fill the mind
    And drive the dark thoughts out.

You'll feel the tension lessening
    And worries fade away
As you ply aching muscles through
    The work-rewarding day.

The chances are you'll wind up
    With a clearer point of view,
And those troubles will seem smaller
    For that work you found to do.

Knowing You Are There

Just knowing you are there, not far away,
Though life piles busy day on busy day
So that I seldom see you—still I know
That I can call and hear your warm "Hello."
My load is lighter knowing that you care,
And I am not alone, for you are there.

New England

Some part of me there is that claims this land,
Its gently rolling hills, its peaceful wood,
Its steeples pointing white against the skies,
Its simple air of quiet hardihood.

There is a part of me that answers to
The cry of seagull as it dips and soars;
The waves' unceasing roll, the ebbing tide,
The dunes of shifting sands along these shores.

Some part of me, though western born and bred,
No matter where this wide land I may roam,
Finds here a strange ancestral pull that draws,
And in New England feels it has come home.

Little Girl Grown

Little girl grown with your laughing eyes,
So young, so eager, so old, so wise!
So filled with exuberant confidence, sure
That life will bring only the best to your door;
Impatient to meet this old world face to face,
So sure you can make it a far better place.

God give you the strength and the courage to do
All life will demand to make those dreams come true,
The strength and the courage, but faith above all,
Should some of those dream castles tumble and fall.

I wish I could hold you. I would if I could,
But life calls you now, and it's right that it should.
I pray they were good seeds—those seeds I have sown—
Now go—and God bless you—my little girl grown.

Mothers

Mothers blow noses,
　　And kiss hurts away;
Make you take naps
　　When you'd much rather play;
Come to your school plays
　　And think you were great;
Make you eat all
　　Of the food on your plate.
Mothers like roses
　　And hate snakes and mice;
Wear pretty dresses
　　And always smell nice;

Sing while they're working,
　　But worry a lot;
Cry when they're happy,
　　But not when they're not;
Think up new games
　　When you're sick in bed;
Tell if you're better
　　By feeling your head;
Bake cakes on birthdays,
　　And trim Christmas trees—
I guess you could say
　　Mothers make memories.

Life in a Parsonage

I've lived in a parsonage all of my life,
As a "preacher's kid" and a minister's wife.
When I was a youngster I thought it was great,
Although most were in a deplorable state.
Sometimes they were sprawling, with rooms of our own.
What unbounded luxury—sleeping alone!
Sometimes they were tiny, but Mom made us fit.
It wasn't as much fun in those, I'll admit.
The rugs that we had were too big or too small;
We folded the too-big ones under, that's all.
Our curtains and drapes seemed never to fit,
But we lowered the rods or raised them a bit.
The rooms needed paint, the wallpaper was bad,
The linoleum always looked pretty sad.
But nobody bothered to do anything,
Since, likely, we'd be moving on in the spring.
There never was money to make a repair—
I wonder that Mom didn't lose faith in prayer.
But we learned to take everything in our stride
And Mom made them homes we could live in with pride.
Moving was always exciting and new
With a new home and new friends to look forward to.
We'd roll out the barrel and start packing dishes,
And Mom must have tucked in a few fervent wishes.

Our parsonage homes have improved with the years.
We no longer live like those first pioneers.
But there's still no money for major repairs
And we have to depend on the Board and our prayers.
We're still very near to the church, for they say
It's ever so much more convenient that way.
Convenient, yes—that we must admit,
But I sometimes wonder for whose benefit.
To show you how handy a parsonage can be,
Last week they borrowed my coffee, my tea;
They borrowed some Band-aids when someone got hurt,
A needle and thread to sew somebody's skirt;
They borrowed my candles, my silver tea tray,
And took down my living room drapes for a play.
The Sunday school's outgrown its quarters, so now
The parsonage handles the surplus, somehow.
Sometimes I dream of a home of my own
Away from the ringing doorbell and the phone,
With just the right number of rooms and no more,
And none but my family to have to do for,
Still, I am sure, when all's said and done,
I'd miss the close ties and the informal fun.
Life in a parsonage—that's all I've had,
But I think I would say the good outweighs the bad.

Bless This Kitchen

Bless this kitchen, Lord, although
    I'm not the world's best cook,
And I'll admit it doesn't have
    That "ideal kitchen" look.

The floor around the high chair—well,
    You know how babies are,
And there's the usual trail of crumbs
    Around the cookie jar.

Those droopy dandelions
    Are a gift of love and sun
From Susie—she's my three-year-old,
    The nature-loving one.

That tin can full of water
    There on the window sill,
Contains some lovely tadpoles
    From the pond across the hill.

The box of dirt beside it
    Has a penny planted, so
My son, the ardent TV fan,
    Can watch his money grow.

The crayon-tablet-paper art
    Here, there and everywhere
On every spot of wall that might
    Have once been clean and bare—

They represent the proud but dubious
    Efforts of my three—
Bless their hearts, they got their
    Inartistic touch from me.

Bless this little kitchen, Lord,
    And keep it safe, I pray,
A warm and happy haven through
    Another busy day.

Lib?

I may not look so nifty,
But I'm very, very thrifty,
I pride myself on being penny-wise.
I'm not silly or flirtatious,
I wear sweaters, but they're spacious,
And I've never been accused of making eyes.

I'm strong and I'm efficient
And extremely self-sufficient.
I can change a tire or repair the sink;
I'm not coy, I never flatter,
I've no use for female patter—
I always say exactly what I think.

I'm smart and energetic,
Very healthy and athletic—
I'm told I have a splendid coat of tan.
All in all, my life's well rounded
And my feet securely grounded—
I've everything I want
Except a man.

Signs of Spring

Icicles hang on stubbornly
    Along the patio;
The patch where daffodils should be
    Is four feet deep in snow.

The sparrows scratch dejectedly
    Upon the frozen ground;
The garden huddles stiff and bleak,
    Its buds icicle bound.

The children's snowman stands intact;
    Not one whit has it dwindled;
The fire on the hearth must be
    Continually rekindled.

The calendar serenely states
    That spring is drawing nearer,
But just a violet or two
    Would make the message clearer.

Still, there are signs of spring about;
    They do their best to cheer—
Those clearance sales on winter clothes,
    A sure sign spring is near!

Really!

Think not, my friend,
I listen, all enthralled,
As you drone on
Of troubles you have known.
I find your aches and pains
Quite boring, really;
I'm simply waiting
To relate my own.

Ladies' Choice

Sally in her mini skirt
    Is cute as she can be;
Susan's maxi trails the ground,
    It's quite a sight to see.
Nancy's ruffled midi makes
    Her look demure and shy;
And all those whistles mean
    That hot-pants Peg is passing by.

Shirley wears hers ankle length
    When she wants to beguile,
And Grandma's wedding dress
    That Mary wears is right in style.
Mother's comfortable again
    With skirts below the knee,
And Grandma in her pants suit
    Is as happy as can be.

What's happened? Have the fashion
    Experts had a change of heart
To actually let *women* say
    What styles shall grace the mart?
I must say it's a welcome change
    And suits me to a T.
You wear what you think right for you,
    I'll do the same for me.

The Voice of Experience

He always knows the answers;
    Every ache or pain you've had,
He's suffered in the same way,
    Only his were twice as bad.

He has the panacea
    For all problems, great and small;
No matter what your hangups,
    You can bet he's had them all.

He can tell you from experience
    Exactly how you feel,
And when he's through describing his,
    Your own seem no big deal.

I guess he really fills a need,
    Distasteful though it is,
But just for once, I'd like my pain
    To hurt as bad as his!

'Tis the Day After Christmas

This year upon December twenty-sixth
    I'll hurry down
And visit all the after-Christmas sales
    All over town.

I'll stock up on next year's supply
    Of wrappings, seals and such;
Experience has taught me one can
    Never have too much.

I'll come back home exhausted
    But exulting in my savings,
And revel in my not-so-thrifty
    Neighbors' envious ravings.

They really are fantastic bargains,
    Never underrate them,
But it would help if, come next Christmas,
    I could just locate them.

I never can think what I bought
    Or where I put my store,
And end up every year by going
    Out and buying more.

For Just That Little While

I like to think that on that Christmas Night,
As Mary held her newborn little one,
For just that little while she could forget
He was the King of Kings and God's own Son.

I like to think that she and Joseph there
Looked on their child as all new parents do,
More than a little awed at what they saw—
The miracle of birth—their dream come true.

I think she must have held His little hand,
And stroked His cheek and counted tiny toes,
And laughed aloud when Joseph, teasing, said
That it was plain the baby had her nose.

I like to think, before the shepherds came,
And great kings knelt and angels sang for joy,
For just that little while she could forget
And love Him for Himself—her baby Boy.

Make a Joyful Noise

Make a joyful noise! The Good Book
    Says it many ways—
Serve with joy and gladness,
    Be generous with praise.

Wear a cheerful countenance,
    Rejoice in joy of others;
Let your speaking be with grace,
    Regard all men as brothers.

Love your neighbor as yourself,
    Speak evil of no one;
With dignity and pride go forth
    To meet each morning's sun.

Seek the true and beautiful,
    Let not your heart be sad;
Do good to them that hate you,
    Love the good, despise the bad.

Make a joyful noise, and sing
    A new song every day—
And may God's peace and joy and love
    Go with you all the way.